FOREWORD

The training methods described in this book have been used for over 35 years, on tens of thousands of dogs. The methods have changed over the years, and these methods work. But they only work if you put in the time and effort. You will probably have your dog for the next ten to 15 years. So remember, a trained dog means a happier dog and a happier owner! Training takes the cooperation of the entire family. No one is going to do the training for you. I am sure that after a hard day's work the last thing you want to hear is how bad your dog was all day. So everyone in the family must become part of the program. Every owner of every breed of dog starts out at the same place as you are. If you are going to ask the assistance of a professional dog trainer, make sure he/she is just that—a professional. Ask for qualifications and recommendations. Watch how they train. Then, if you are satisfied with the instructor, ask your veterinarian if he/she has ever heard of the trainer. Your dog is like your child. He is a member of your family. So in choosing a professional trainer, use the same criteria you would in choosing a day camp or a baby-sitter. Dog training is one of the most interesting fields an individual can get into. There are always new theories and new methods. There are so many different types of dog training that you never stop learning. I learn every day, whether from reading books like this one, watching other trainers, going to seminars or just talking to people. So good luck...it's really not that hard!

Author Dan Gentile, Jr. poses with one of his prize students. Mr. Gentile, who has educational training from the United States Armed Forces Institute, Cornell University of Veterinary Medicine and Ontario Veterinary College, has been professionally training dogs in all phases of obedience since the 1960s.

FOLLOW THE LEADER

Over the years, dogs have earned the name "Man's Best Friend" for good reason—a well-trained, well-behaved dog can truly be one of your closest companions. Dogs don't judge always *one* leader and the same holds true for your dog. Your family is his pack—a pack where, just like his ancestors, there is only *one* leader. That leader must be you. When your dog enters

A well-trained, well-behaved dog can be one of your closest companions. Teaching your dog to obey simple commands such as heeling (shown) starts your dog toward earning the status of "best friend."

you, or put demands on you. They simply become your trusted friends. But it takes time, patience, and understanding on your part to teach your dog how to earn the status of "best friend."

Your dog's closest ancestor is the wolf, an animal that has run wild in packs for the past 10,000 years. In each wolfpack, there is your home for the first time, you must show him that everyone else in the household has a higher position of authority.

THINKING LIKE A DOG

To be the leader, you must train your dog by actually thinking like a dog. Your dog does not think of you as a human, but

The first and most important aspect of training your dog is to establish yourself as the leader. Your dog must look up to you for guidance and obey your every command.

Playing tug-of-war and roughhousing with your dog is fun but can be disastrous to your training program. Every time your dog "wins" he has established himself as the leader—the exact opposite of what you are trying to accomplish.

wins. Even by simply turning away when you are tired of playing, your dog thinks you have given up and he runs away victorious, and takes one step up the rung of leadership.

When puppies become too rough, their mothers correct them by either shaking them by the scruff of the neck, holding their mouths closed, growling, or staring them straight in the eyes until they give in and turn away. You can gain control of your dog using the same techniques because your pet understands

Correct an unruly dog by holding him down with one hand on his neck and the other on his side until he submits to you by raising his rear leg. This is an exercise that should be repeated by everyone in the household to establish the dog's place in the "pack."

as another dog, so you must communicate with him on a level he understands. For example, your dog will try to become the leader of your household by play-biting or tug-of-war. When you play tug-of-war, or roughhouse with your pup, it seems like cute behavior, especially when your dog is a puppy, but every time you play tug-of-war or roughhouse with your dog, he and responds to these forms of instinctual discipline.

The leader of the pack corrects the unruly puppy or young wolf by standing on his chest (pinning him on the ground) with its mouth on the pup's throat until he submits. Again, you can practice a similar maneuver with your dog by holding him down with his legs facing away from you and placing one hand on his neck, the other on his side until he submits to you, the leader, by raising his rear leg. In fact, every member of your family (your dog's pack) should perform this discipline to ensure that your pup knows who's the top dog!

Your dog may nudge you with his nose in an effort to make you pet him. If you submit to this exploitive conduct, you can spoil the dog. Make the dog earn your affection by having him sit or lie down before being petted.

owners by nudging them with their nose, head, body, or paw so they can be petted. But the dog wants more than your hand on his fur. He is saying "Stop what you are doing immediately and pay attention to me!" Constantly petting or spoiling the dog is an easy way dominant dogs learn to become the leader, because in the pack all the members constantly lick and touch the leader. If your dog wants to be petted, let him earn it by first having him sit or lie down.

EARNING AFFECTION

Although it is often hard to resist petting your pup just because he's a lovable, adorable addition to your household, he must learn that he has got to earn your love. Dogs often try to take advantage of their

THE IMPORTANCE OF TRAINING

Thinking like your dog is merely the first step to becoming the leader. Obedience training is the sure way to show your dog that you are in control. Once in control, your dog will follow you, the leader, throughout his life in the special place in your family reserved just for him.

THE PROPER EQUIPMENT

Before you start your dog's obedience training, you must purchase the proper equipment. Imagine sending your children off to school without pencils or notebooks or lunch money. They would be totally unprepared. Your dog must also start his "schooling" with the proper supplies, namely, a chain training collar or prong/pressure collar, a 6-foot leash, a 25-foot leash and a small tab to attach to his collar. Let's take a closer look at each piece of equipment.

CHAIN TRAINING COLLAR

Once you begin training, the only correction you will ever give your dog is a snap on the collar, so you want as much control as possible in a collar that is dependable. The best chain collars are those that have the least space between each link, and are heavy enough so as not to break. Measure your dog's neck and purchase a collar that is 2 to 3 inches larger than his neck size. Small dogs (up to 25 pounds) generally require a 12- to 14-inch collar. Medium dogs (25 to 40 pounds) should fit into a 16-inch collar, and larger dogs may require a collar that is 18 or more inches in length.

To correctly place the training collar on your dog, hold one of the rings in your left hand and drop the chain through that ring so that when you pick up the collar it is in the shape of a "P." Next, while your dog is seated on your left side, place the collar over his neck with the running part of the chain (the portion that slides easily) on top of the neck. Putting a collar on your dog may seem pretty self-explanatory, but if you place the collar on incorrectly, the chain will not give when you jerk it and will constrict your dog's neck.

PRONG/PRESSURE COLLAR

If you have a large dog that does not respond to the standard chain training collar (or if you just need some extra strength), use a prong/pressure collar. However, if your dog is aggressive, I do not

The training collar is the first purchase you must make before you begin training. Be sure to measure your dog's neck for proper fit and buy a collar with close links (right) as opposed to wide links (left).

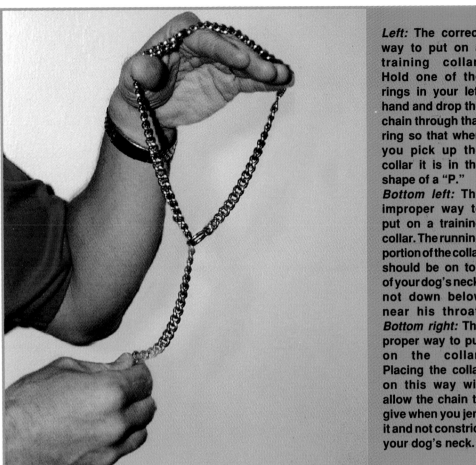

Left: The correct way to put on a training collar. Hold one of the rings in your left hand and drop the chain through that ring so that when you pick up the collar it is in the shape of a "P."

Bottom left: The improper way to put on a training collar. The running portion of the collar should be on top of your dog's neck, not down below near his throat.

Bottom right: The proper way to put on the collar. Placing the collar on this way will allow the chain to give when you jerk it and not constrict your dog's neck.

recommend this kind of collar because it can heighten aggression.

While these collars may look as if they are painful to your dog, they actually place less stress on the dog's neck because they evenly apply pressure. Standard chain training collars apply pressure at only one point on the neck, where the chain slips through the ring.

To put a prong/ pressure collar on your dog, remove just enough links so that when you pull up on the large ring, the chain forms a triangle. As your dog grows, add links to ensure that you are applying pressure to his neck. Once your dog is fully trained on the prong/pressure collar, you can always go back to using the standard chain collar.

The proper fitting of the prong/ pressure collar. This type of collar may look dangerous but in actuality is very safe, comfortable, and effective for large, aggressive breeds.

LEASHES

You will need two leashes: a 25-foot cotton or nylon leash, about $5/8$ of an inch wide (sometimes called a lunge line) and a 6-foot training leash. For smaller dogs, look for a $1/2$ an inch to $3/4$ of an inch wide, 6-foot leash. Large dogs require a double nylon 1-inch wide leash or a $3/4$ of an inch to 1-inch wide heavy leather leash.

TRAINING TAB

While not actually training your dog when he is off-leash, when he is walking around your house or yard, you will still want to have control over him. Remember, the only correction you will ever give your pet is by jerking his collar. So, when he is off-leash, it can be difficult to find the small ring on his training collar to correct him. A small tab—a 3-inch piece of an old leash will work fine— dangling from his collar at all times will allow you to easily reach over and correct any unwanted behavior.

THE BASICS

While shopping for your basic training supplies, you will surely see lots of other equipment on the market—such as head halters, leather collars, and remote control collars. But don't worry, what I have outlined above is really all you will need to get started on your own obedience training program.

GETTING YOUR DOG'S ATTENTION

The first step in gaining control over your dog—becoming the leader!—is to get his undivided attention. To use another school day's analogy,

The purpose of our first training step—getting your dog's attention—is to have your pet focus completely on your body without you having to say one

The author demonstrates the proper way of getting your dog's attention. Allow the dog to reach the end of the 25-foot line, then give a sharp snap on the line and walk in the opposite direction. Do not talk to or praise the dog—just keep your eyes on him.

consider how hard it is for a young girl or boy to listen to their teacher discuss the multiplication tables when all they are thinking about is playing with their friends after class. The teacher has to first get their attention, and your young untrained pup is no different.

word. Once you have his undivided attention, you have the foundation for all basic training exercises.

HE GOES ONE WAY, YOU GO THE OTHER

To teach your dog how to pay attention to you, attach the 25-foot lunge line to his training

Getting your dog's attention. Every time your dog walks one way, you walk the other while snapping on the leash. Continue this until your dog follows you every time you turn around.

collar and take him to a large, grassy area. Let him run whichever way he wants, while you walk in the opposite direction. As soon as he reaches the end of the 25-foot line, give him a sharp snap and keep moving in the opposite direction. While performing this exercise, do not talk to or praise your dog, just keep your eyes on him. Each time your dog walks one way, you walk the other. Continue this until every time you turn around, your dog follows you. Gradually reel in the leash until he is right around you and then stop.

   Once your dog is perfect in one location—you will know he's perfect when he is always at

your feet watching for your next move—take him to another location where there are plenty of distractions, like other dogs, children, joggers, or ball players. It is ideal to work your dog in locations where you think he would bolt if he were off-leash. You can even cause your own problems—by having someone throw a ball to distract your dog so he will run in the opposite direction from you—so you can correct the problem before it actually happens. You can only progress to the next training step when your dog is perfect in three or more locations that

Eventually your dog will begin to follow you without the snap. Gradually reel in the leash until he is close to you and then stop. The next training session you can try the same exercise in a location where there are distractions.

have as many distractions as possible.

KEEPING IT INTERESTING

While performing this exercise, you will undoubtedly find that your pup will get his feet caught up in the 25-foot leash, but keep moving. All you need to do is give him enough slack so he can walk himself out of the tangle. Never stop to untangle him because if you do, he will get exactly what he wants and that is for you to stop the exercise.

Your pet may also try to display his boredom of the exercise by taking the leash in his mouth. If he does, just give him a slight snap—emphasis on *slight*, because you don't want to break his jaw. If that correction doesn't work, take him to a different location where there are enough distractions that he will forget about the 25-foot line and concentrate on the children playing, the joggers, or the ballplayers.

Example of the left about turn on heel. Notice that the lead is held close to the dog's neck to avoid tangling.

If your dog continually jumps up on you as you are moving, reel up the line and give him a hard correction (a quick snap on the collar), and continue making your turns. Remember, you go one way, he goes the other.

THERE'S A LIMIT

As with all the training exercises, you will soon learn to train your dog for only ten minutes twice a day or once a day for 15 to 20 minutes. Longer training sessions don't mean better training sessions. If your dog is perfect in five minutes at one location, stop the lesson. Next time take him to one of your alternative training locations.

The more locations with the most distractions will ensure that your dog is actively paying attention to you. Once your pup follows you with his body—no matter which direction you walk—you can begin to praise him.

HEEL

Once you have your dog's undivided attention around a number of distractions, you are ready to progress to the next step—teaching him to heel. Heel simply means that the dog is walking on your left side with your left leg between his head and shoulder blade. (In case you're wondering, dogs are trained to heel on the left so animal handlers around the world have a standard with which to work.)

GETTING STARTED

Before you begin any lesson, always be sure that the dog's training collar is on correctly—with the running part of the chain (the part that moves) going over the dog's neck. Next, attach the 6-foot leash to his collar,

Before you begin a training session, make sure the collar is correctly placed on the dog's neck—with the running part (the part that moves) over the dog's neck.

hold the leash with two hands until the snap is loose and begin to walk. It doesn't matter if you start off with your left foot or your right foot, just say, "Heel," and walk with your dog on your left side. Keep your eyes on him and praise him verbally only when he is in the correct heel position.

GIVING THE HEEL COMMAND

Only give the heel command

once. After that, your only interaction with your pup is to either praise him verbally or correct him with a quick snap on his leash. Also, never use your dog's name before any command except "Come." If your dog doesn't enjoy taking your commands, such as the "sit," "down," and "stay" commands, he may begin to dislike the sound of his name as well. Only use his name in conjunction with something he enjoys, such as coming to you, eating, or playing.

CORRECTING COMMON PROBLEMS

You will most likely run into a few minor yet very typical problems while teaching your dog to heel. If your dog gets overly excited when you praise him, simply continue walking and correct him by quickly snapping on his leash. If he goes over to your right side, snap him over to your left. If he gets tangled in the leash, keep moving and give him enough slack so he can walk out of the tangle on his own.

If the dog lags behind, give him a quick snap on the leash and encourage him to stay with you by praising him verbally. If the opposite occurs—if his shoulder goes past your left leg—it indicates that your dog is not paying attention to you. To regain his attention, make a 180-degree right turn while snapping on the leash so the dog will have to follow your direction. Another sure-fire correction is to turn 180 degrees to your left. You will inevitably step directly into your dog because he is not paying attention to where you are walking. The best dog I ever trained to heel was the one I literally fell on, because from that point on he *always* watched me to make sure I wouldn't fall on him again! So, when you walk into your dog do not stop or apologize, just keep moving.

Students of the author's training school practice the heel. The heel command should be given only once. After that, the only interaction with your dog should be either verbal praise or a quick leash correction.

A proud owner and dog demonstrate the heel. Walk with your dog on your left side, keep your eyes on him and praise only when he is in the correct heel position.

ALL EYES ON YOU

One other very effective way of ensuring that your dog's attention is focused solely on you is to suddenly run backward (while facing your dog) and praise the dog to come to you. Snap the leash to keep him to your left, and when he reaches the proper heel position, move forward in the original direction you were going and, once again, say, "Heel." In essence, when you make a right turn, left turn, run backward, or go forward all within a matter of minutes, the dog has no choice but to pay attention to your body.

Remember, the only interaction you will have with your pup during the heel exercise is either verbal praise, or correction by a quick snap on the leash. Each time you snap the leash, you knock your dog's confidence down a peg, so praise him after he corrects his behavior to help build back his spirit. Your dog cannot reason and does not know right from wrong. It is up to you to teach him what is right (by praising him verbally) and what is wrong (by a quick snap and likes to do homework?) and you allowed him to quit by stopping your movement.

However, whenever you wish to stop the exercise for a moment, slow down your pace with your last few steps so the dog knows that it is time to stop. Otherwise, he may keep moving past you. When you do come to a complete stop, give

An owner and dog who have advanced to heeling off-lead. This is accomplished only after you are certain that you have complete control of your dog in all situations.

release on the leash). Be firm, but never cruel.

STAYING IN CHARGE

Regardless of whether you are correcting or praising your dog, always keep moving! If you stop walking at any time to, for example, wait for him to keep up with your pace or get himself out of a tangled leash, your dog wins. He wanted to end the exercise (who

your pup lots of physical and verbal praise. Then, when it comes time to start again, just say, "Heel." Whether you walk slow, fast, or jog, the dog still has to keep pace with you.

Once your dog heels perfectly in one location, practice in two or three more areas with as many distractions as possible to make sure that your pup has given you his complete attention.

Proper heeling technique is required and judged in dog shows. This is the most basic procedure of the show dog handler.

SIT

Now that your dog has mastered the heel exercise, it is time to take his training a step further by teaching him to sit on command. The sit command is very important because it will help calm your dog if he gets too excited, and prevent him from

WORKING WITH TREATS

Before you begin training your dog to sit, try this test. Walk over to him with his favorite tasty treat in your hand and let him smell the morsel. Then simply hold it up over his head in front of his eyes. When he looks up to see the food

After mastering the heel command, you may proceed to teach your dog the command to sit. This is an important command as it will help to calm your dog when he becomes too excited.

jumping up on you and your guests. As with all the exercises we have discussed, your dog must learn to sit on your command *around a number of distractions.*

he will automatically sit in order to keep the treat in his line of vision.

It helps speed things along if your dog is hungry when you

begin your sit lesson. To start training with treats, perform the same exercise mentioned above but be careful not to hold the food so high that your dog has to jump up to get it. Once he sits, praise him—"Good Boy!"—and reward him with a treat. After he sits a few times when you hold the treat above his head, actually say the word "Sit." As soon as he sits, give him the treat. If you try this a few times, your dog will sit every time you give the command because he expects his treat.

A LITTLE PRAISE GOES A LONG WAY

When you begin the lesson, reward your dog with a treat each time he sits, then every other time, then every third time, and so on until he forgets all about the tasty treats and sits merely by hearing the sound of your voice. Once he is perfect, his only reward will be your verbal praise—and dogs live for food, shelter, affection and pleasing their masters!

When you praise your dog don't pet him too much because he will start to think that *he* is the leader. Remember, in dog and wolf packs the pups constantly touch their leaders. So you, as the leader, should pet your dog no more than three times, all the while telling him how good he is. In addition, when *anyone* wants to pet your dog, always make him sit first—let him earn the reward of affection. If he gets up and starts jumping, ask the person to stop petting him and correct the dog with a snap on the leash so he will sit. Only then can he be

This dog is sitting happily while being praised by her owner. When beginning to teach the sit command, reward your dog with a treat and praise, then gradually teach him to sit without the treats. Eventually your dog will sit on your command.

petted again. Essentially if you want to solve any problem with your dog, cause the problem. Ask strangers, friends, or children to pet your dog to see if he will listen to you and remain seated or disobey you and jump up. If he jumps up, correct him by snapping the leash. Your dog should *always* sit when you tell him so, regardless if dogs, squirrels, children, or birds are playing around him.

Treats are effective when teaching new commands. Very small tasty treats, such as hot dog slices, are ideal in the beginning phases of training.

first and then progress to the leash once he knows the sit command. Here's how the leash correction for the sit command works. While walking in the heel position, as you are about to stop, take your right hand and place it under where your left hand is on the leash (you should be holding the leash so the snap at the end is slightly loose). Slow down your pace before you actually stop, remove your left hand from the leash and place your left thumb and middle finger in front of your dog's hips. Gently squeeze your two fingers while placing a slight downward pressure on your dog's lower back. Do not push down too hard because your dog will try to

One of the reasons that you teach the sit is to prevent your dog from jumping up on people. Immediately enforce the sit command whenever your dog jumps up on you or someone else.

A PERSONAL TIP ABOUT TREATS

Over the years, I have found that dogs just love hot dogs as treats. Maybe it's because they share the same name, or maybe it's just an elusive "human" food, but dogs go crazy over them. When I train my dogs, I take one whole hot dog, cut it into dime-size slices, and cook it in the microwave on high for five minutes. When it is finished, I put it in the freezer for about five minutes, to take away some of the heat. There you have it—the perfect dog treat (remember, it's not a meal) in ten minutes!

SITTING FROM THE HEEL POSITION

Leash correction is another way to teach your dog to sit and if you wish, you can always use treats

You can teach your dog to sit from the heel. Simply slow down to a stop, place your left thumb and middle finger in front of your dog's hips, and squeeze while placing a downward pressure on the dog's lower back. Pull up on the leash as shown and say "Sit" as you push down on the dog's backside.

move his rear end to get away from your hand. While pushing downward, snap up with the leash so that you are now holding in your right hand and say, "Sit."

Praise your pup both verbally and physically as soon as he sits. However, if he gets up or starts to jump up while you are praising him, immediately stop your praise, snap up with the leash and say, "No! Sit."

USING ONLY THE LEASH

After you have successfully gotten your dog to sit a few times and are confident that he understands the word "Sit," you no longer need to apply pressure with your left hand when you stop moving. All you need to do at this point is snap the leash up, say, "sit"—only once—and give him lots of praise when he completes the command. However, if he doesn't sit on the first command, simply snap up on the leash and say "No!" at the same time, praising him only when he sits. Remember, you only say, "Sit" once, after that you are either verbally praising your dog or correcting him with a "No!" followed by a snap on the leash.

Placing slight pressure on your dog's lower back helps communicate the sit command. Do not push down too hard or else the dog will move his rear end to get away from your hand. Be sure to praise during training and eventually your dog will sit on command without your help.

JUST SAY "NO!"

To progress the exercise even further, do not say, "Sit" the next time you come to a complete stop. If your dog doesn't automatically sit, correct him by snapping the leash and say "No!" at the same time. If he still doesn't sit, snap the leash again while saying "No!" until he sits. Your dog will soon understand that "No!" said in a firm but not cruel voice means that whatever he is doing is wrong and he must stop immediately. As you go through this program, you will discover that "No!" will be used in every single exercise to correct your dog after you have given him the initial command.

THE LEADER OF THE PACK

When your dog sits at your command, he understands that *you* are the leader of the pack. He knows that each and every time you stop he must obey you—the leader—and sit at your left side. He understands that if he does not sit when you stop, he will displease you and receive a correction. He can only earn your praise by being obedient and sitting on command.

STAY

As you and your student progress from heel to sit and on to stay, you will notice that you are gaining much more control over your dog. The stay command lets you do the activities you used to do before you brought home your new, four-legged family addition. You will be able to talk to friends without the annoyance of having your dog jump up on them, and you'll be able to eat, read, or watch television in peace, even while your pup is in the same room.

LET'S STAY

As we work our way to the formal stay command, I would like to point out that you have already taught your dog how to

The author gives the hand signal to "Stay." This command allows you to do the activities you used to do before you had a dog. At this point in training, you will begin to notice that you are gaining control of your dog.

stay in the sit exercise. Think about it. Each time your pet got up from his sitting position, you corrected him by snapping up with the leash while saying "No!"

To begin, while your dog is in the heel position on the 6-foot leash, put the tab on his collar and leave it there from this point on. Hold your left hand, palm open, in front of his face and say, "Stay." Slack off on the leash, and while facing your dog take two steps back and remain in that spot for about 30 seconds. Next, return to your dog while reeling up the leash but be careful not to pull the leash or your dog will move. When you are back at the heel position, give him lots of praise—he earned it if he listened to your stay command and didn't move a muscle. Continue the exercise until you are eventually at the end of the leash—a full 6 feet away from your pup—and he is sitting and staying and listening to your every command. If he doesn't move while you are at the end of the leash, praise him with a soft tone while remaining 6 feet away from him. If you are using treats for training, always give your dog a treat whenever you return to the spot where he stayed.

If your dog gets up at *any* time during the sit exercise, run to him, snap up on the leash or tab

Finally, make him "stay" for long periods of time, even up to an hour. He doesn't have to stand the entire time he is staying; even if he lies down, he is still obeying you by not moving from his spot. And don't worry, you don't have to stand and watch the motionless pup for an hour— make him stay while you are

This owner and dog are practicing the "Sit-Stay" command. Notice that there is slack on the leash, about a six-foot distance between dog and owner, and the owner is praising.

and say, "No! Sit. Stay." Likewise, if he runs across the training area, snap him back to his original spot, while snapping on the leash or tab and saying, "No" all the way back. Don't pull or drag him, simply snap him back, leave him at his original place, and say, "Sit. Stay."

When your dog remains perfectly still on the 6-foot leash, proceed to the 25-foot leash.

eating, watching television, talking on the phone, etc. Just keep in mind that if he moves, stop what you are doing and *immediately* run over and correct him.

THE IMPORTANCE OF THE TAB

Your pup should be wearing the tab on his collar at all times because it can be cumbersome to leave his leash on while he is in your home. However, if your dog consistently runs away from you in the house, leave the leash on for a few days until he starts to obey. If you are practicing stay in your kitchen, for example, and he gets up, all you need to do is walk over and pull the tab. Groping for the ring on the end of the collar can be frustrating and time-consuming; the dog could be out the door by the time you grab the ring.

DISTRACTIONS, DISTRACTIONS, DISTRACTIONS

As with every lesson we have discussed, your dog must stay in as many different areas with as

Using both the verbal command and a hand signal to "Stay" will reinforce the teaching of the command and can effectively speed up the learning process.

Once you have mastered the stay command while alone with your dog, continue training in a park or other area that provides distractions. This will teach your dog to ignore exciting sights, smells, and sounds while concentrating on your commands.

many different distractions as you can find. Take him to parks with lots of joggers or children or other dogs. If he will have nothing to do with you when you practice stay, don't get discouraged. Just start from the beginning by getting his attention. Finally, if you find yourself losing your patience because your dog doesn't seem to understand anything you are saying, back up a bit and have him perform one of the exercises that he has already perfected. You will feel better because your dog will prove to you that your hard work has paid off. And, your dog will feel better because he will earn your praise!

DOWN—THE MAGIC COMMAND

When your dog follows your down command, it confirms his suspicion: he is the lowest of the low, the bottom of the heap, the most inconsequential member of the pack. This is exactly what you want. When he is down on his belly, he is completely vulnerable to everything and everyone. No wonder down is the hardest command to teach! Once mastered, however, down is the best command to help reduce a dog's aggressiveness.

Before you teach your dog to go down, he must react perfectly to all other commands learned so far: heel, sit, and stay. He must also respond perfectly to every member of your family—his pack. Once the down command is learned, the rest of his training should be easy because he will most likely perform other commands with little hesitation. In his view, any command is better than down.

The down command is the hardest to teach but the most effective in reducing a dog's aggressiveness. In teaching this command, you must use a "hands-on" approach as demonstrated by the author in this photo.

THE BASIC DOWN EXERCISE

Put your dog on your left side with him sitting in the heel position. You should both face the same direction. Hold the leash taut in your right hand on your right side, level with your waist. Now, slide your left hand, palm down, along the leash to your dog's neck.

Next, take the entire leash in your left hand and get down on your left knee. Reach across yourself with your right hand, put it under your dog's right front leg and grab his left front ankle (a yoga position?).

While holding his ankle, lift his front legs slightly with your right arm. At the same time, press his back lightly with your left elbow and say, "Down." Kaboom! You and your dog tumble to the floor because you didn't do this fast enough; your dog has lifted his right foot a bit, loosening your grip. Try again. As soon as your dog goes all the way to the ground, release the pressure on his collar and his back. Say, "Stay," and stand up, if you can. If he gets up when you do, repeat the whole exercise until you both get it right.

A MORE ADVANCED DOWN METHOD

When you and your dog have perfected the previous method, down command becomes easier. As described above, hold the leash snugly in your right hand, slide your left hand down the leash to the collar, palm down, push down on the collar with your left hand and say, "Down." Voila! He assumes the down position. Immediately release the pressure on his neck, give him the stay command, stand up, and walk to the end of the leash keeping an eye on the dog.

This is not the way to teach the down command. Your dog cannot understand pointing and will become confused by the action.

A more advanced method of teaching the down is to do so with the leash and collar. This method should only be attempted after mastering the basic down command.

If your dog stands up at the down command after (you think) he has learned it perfectly, the only way to correct him is to first snap up on the leash, saying, "No!" then snap down on the leash and say, "Down." If he has the audacity to get up and run across the training area, snap him back to the exact spot he left (don't drag him) saying, "No!" It is important to show him who is boss now or you could lose this one. You must snap up on the leash first because that is the correction for sit, which he must do before going down. Sitting removes his two back legs from the contest with you, giving you a distinct advantage. If he were standing up, he could resist with you on all four legs, not just two.

DOWN—WITH TREATS

Just as with the other commands, you can teach "down" using treats. Ask him to sit while you hold the treat slightly in front of and above his nose. Give him the treat when you have his attention.

PRAISE IS POWERFUL!

Remember to give your dog lots of praise when he follows your commands. If he gets excited about your praise, he may stand up when he is in the down position. This is an opportunity for you to confront and correct the problem while he is

A picnic, parade, or other event where a number of people are congregating is an excellent place to teach your dog to stay amidst distractions.

Do this again, but bring the treat slowly to the ground before you give it to him. As he sits, contemplating a delicious snack, his eyes and head will follow the treat. Finally, offer the treat as you put it between his front legs and reward him with it if he follows it to a down position. To advance even further, hold a treat on the ground in front of your dog. Guide him to the down position, saying, "Down."

still in training. Give the "down" command again, letting him know that down *always* means down/stay, just as sit *always* means sit/stay. In all circumstances, he must stay down.

Don't get discouraged or lose patience with your pet. The training sessions and your dog's ultimate obedience will result in a strong bond between you. He will understand that you are the leader and his role is that of your loyal follower.

Above: These dogs are in a training class that is practicing the down command with distractions. *Below:* Another class performs the down command around a human distraction. It is very important that you teach your dog to obey your commands regardless of what is around him, so be sure to train in areas that will expose your dog to all kinds of distractions.

COME—THE FUN COMMAND

Since your first lesson, you have been teaching your dog to come to you on command. Remember, when you taught your dog to follow your body, and later trained him to heel, you ran backwards to get his attention so he would follow you and to come to you.

voice, "Spot. Come!"—as if you just won the lottery.

GETTING STARTED

To begin, have your dog sit and stay at the end of the 6-foot leash in an area with distractions. With a happy tone, say his name and then, "Come." While running

"Come" is the only command that you should use in conjunction with your dog's name. Never, ever use the come command to punish your dog.

Before we begin, keep in mind that when you call your dog to come to you, it should *always be fun!* Why should your dog come running to you if you are going to punish him? When you call your dog, say it with excitement in your

backwards, give a slight tug on his leash. As he runs towards you, reel up the leash, all the while praising him. If he starts to go over to either your left or right side, just keep running backward so that he remains directly in front of you.

This sequence demonstrates the teaching of the come command.

Top left: First, have your dog sit.

Top right: Then, give the command to stay.

Right: Finally, walk backward away from your dog and give the command "Come" in a pleasant tone.

When your pup gets to you, guide him into the sit position directly in front of you (facing you), either by saying "Sit" or slightly snapping up with the leash. Lavish him with praise only when he sits and, if he happens to get up from the sitting position when you are praising him, or at any time, just say, "No!" Stop praising him and snap up on his collar. If you have been using treats to train your pet, give him one as soon as he sits.

MOVING ON

Once your dog is perfect on the 6-foot leash, move on up to the 25-foot leash. To take the come exercise a step further, find an enclosed area and let your pup run around with the leash dragging behind him and basically pay little attention to him. When you get to a position where you can correct him if he doesn't listen to your command, say his name and "Come." Crouch down with your arms extended while praising him to come to you. If he doesn't run or walk to you ,

The come command should be the most enjoyable of the basic commands for you and your dog. When your dog gets to you, guide him into the sit position directly in front of you.

immediately, regardless of the number of distractions around him, reach down and give the leash a quick snap and say "No!"

FUN GAMES

This particular exercise should be more enjoyable for both you and your dog than the other commands we have covered. For example, you can teach the come command by playing hide and seek with your dog. Hide behind a tree or a bush and let your pet find you. When he spots you and runs to you (comes), praise him when he is sitting directly at your feet. If he gets distracted or looks but cannot find you, call his name again and run from your hiding place and away from him. Dogs love to chase and follow their masters so you can bet that he will playfully romp after you. When he "catches" you, have him sit and praise him.

If your dog is a ball player, you can teach him to come by bouncing the ball in front of him

This is a demonstration of the come command while off lead. The owner is running backward to encourage a faster recall by the dog.

while he is staying. Call him. When he comes to you, hold the ball over his head so he has to look up at it and sit. Reward him with the ball only after he comes and sits directly in front of you.

You can also use your pup's favorite squeak toy as a training tool. While in an enclosed area, squeak the toy to get his attention and get him excited, then call him using his name. When he comes to you, either give him the toy or, if he is on the 25-foot leash, reward him by throwing it so he can retrieve it for you. If he doesn't bring the toy back to you, run away from him to make him chase you.

REMEMBER THE MAGIC WORD

Always remember that the "come" command should be fun! Devise your own games if you'd like, using toys, treats, or just your own voice. As your dog's leader, you will find that he is loyal to you and will follow you as soon as he hears his name. It just takes a little practice.

OK—THE RELEASE COMMAND

The final reward of everything we have been working on is to simply release your dog—let him go about his business by saying "OK!" When you give the release command, your dog is free to do anything he wants (within reason, of course...). As we discussed in earlier chapters, always have your dog sit before he goes in or out the door, gets into your car, or eats his food. Once he is seated, say "OK!" with excitement in your voice and let him run about.

As an example, have your dog sit and stay in front of your door while he is on the leash. As you exit the house first—because you are the leader—simply say "OK!" meaning that your dog is free to leave the house and doesn't have to heel. However, if he moves before you release him, correct him by snapping up on the leash and saying, "NO!" Try the same exercise before your dog jumps into the car, or prior to giving him a treat or his favorite toy. When you want control over your dog again, just give him a slight snap on the leash to get his attention and move on.

The author demonstrates the release command. This final command allows your dog to do whatever he wants to do. Make your dog sit before he goes in or out the door and always make sure that your yard is safely enclosed.

YEARS OF FUN AND DEVOTION

My final advice to you is to just have fun! Your dog will be a member of your family for the next 15 years or so. So the sooner you get started teaching him the proper way to behave, the sooner he will be transformed into the obedient, devoted pet you have always wanted. The old saying about how hard it is to teach an old dog new tricks isn't just an over-used cliché. Training your pet when he is a pup of four months or so will help ensure that he will listen and respond to your commands for the rest of his life. And that will make everyone happy.

SOCIALIZATION

THE FIRST SIX WEEKS

Socialization is the most important thing an owner can do to enhance his relationship with his dog. During the first six weeks weeks may grow to believe that he is human. (A dog who thinks he is human is the last thing you want!) While he is very young, his

Once you have chosen your puppy, the most important thing you must do is socialize him.

of life, before socialization with humans can begin, it is vital for a puppy to interact with his brothers and sisters.

A puppy who is not exposed to other puppies or dogs in his early mother shows him which behaviors are acceptable and which are not. If he doesn't learn these early lessons, he may become overly dependent upon his owner and become fearful or aggressive with other dogs. To give a puppy time to socialize with his own family, never take him from a litter before he is six weeks old.

SIX TO 14 WEEKS—TIME FOR SOCIALIZATION

Between the ages of six to 14 weeks is a critical period in a puppy's life. This is the time to socialize him by introducing him to various environments, objects and humans. He must give up cuddling with his siblings and realize that the two legged creature holding the leash and bowl will be providing his meals from now on.

Socialization begins at six weeks and must continue through about 14 weeks. Be sure to expose him to a number of different people, objects, and environments while he is still young and impressionable.

Once he is fully vaccinated, expose your puppy to other puppies as well as humans. If he is only exposed to humans, he may think that he is one—and that is the last thing you want him to believe.

Environment and conditioning are everything at this stage of a puppy's life. It is well worth the effort to give your pet a chance to interact and have physical contact with people. If a puppy is well socialized, both he and his owner will reap the benefits. A happy dog and a happy owner can enjoy a rewarding relationship for many years. If a puppy is deprived of socialization, he will grow up fearful of humans and never be well adjusted, a regrettable circumstance.

BRINGING YOUR PUPPY HOME

Before you bring your puppy home, set up an appointment for a physical check-up with your veterinarian. This should include any necessary vaccinations. Make this visit enjoyable for your pet so that future appointments won't be a problem.

If you have properly socialized your dog, he will not fear the veterinarian. This can be done by introducing him to many different people and by making his first visit an enjoyable one.

Above: Socialization includes letting your puppy play with children. Just be sure to supervise these playtimes for the safety of both your dog and the child. *Below:* A properly socialized dog can become an ideal companion for a person whether young or old.

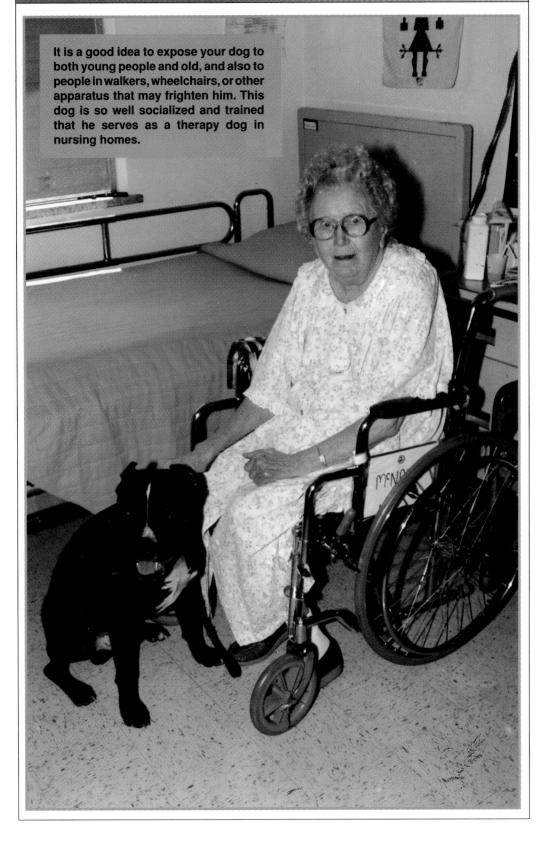

It is a good idea to expose your dog to both young people and old, and also to people in walkers, wheelchairs, or other apparatus that may frighten him. This dog is so well socialized and trained that he serves as a therapy dog in nursing homes.

Take advantage of situations where your puppy can socialize with older dogs who are calm and well trained.

Once his vaccinations are up to date, it is time to expose him to the world at large. Introduce him to as many places, people and situations as possible. For example, let him hear loud noises: trains and whistles, rumbling trucks, thunderstorms, ocean waves, maybe even rock music. Accustom him to walking on various surfaces: grass, concrete, sand, tile.

Most important, let him see people, young and old. Take him to a shopping mall or a park where he'll see all kinds of things: people with hats, beards, umbrellas, sunglasses, wheelchairs, and maybe even some cats. Any place you take him will add to his experience and socialization.

A word of caution: be careful around other dogs; you don't want him to pick up any diseases. Also, be aware that between eight and ten weeks of age, puppies go through a period of apprehension. Be patient and avoid upsetting them at this time.

In addition to different people, your dog should also be exposed to different environments and a variety of walking surfaces. Ideally, you'd like to take your dog to a new place that will be fun for the both of you, such as the beach.

These dogs are not frightened of the horse nor uncomfortable in the snow because they were exposed to both during their socialization period of puppyhood.

HOUSEBREAKING

There's no such thing as an almost housebroken dog. Either he is or he isn't. When a dog is housebroken, he never uses the house for his toilet. Let me say a few words about paper training here. Puppies learn by association. If you allow him to do his duties in the house on paper, you are telling him, in effect, that it is all right to do it within the four walls of the house—you are

Many people do not understand why their dog does not know what to do when taken outside. Merely taking him outside does not mean he knows what he's being taken outside for. The biggest problem between the dog and owner is that the dog would love to please but doesn't know how, and the owner would love to teach the dog but doesn't know how.

Allowing a puppy to do his duties on paper inside the house is telling him that it is okay to eliminate inside the house. If you want your dog to "go" outside, then that is where he must learn to "go" from the very beginning.

making this association in his mind. Later, when you expect him to do his duties outside, he may think you are a little crazy—and you can't blame him. Any healthy pup that is eight weeks of age or older, even in cold weather can go outside. Of course, you don't leave him out long enough to get chilled. You take him out just long enough to do his duties.

In theory, housebreaking is very simple. It is finding a means of preventing the puppy from doing his duties in the house and only giving him an opportunity to do them outside. A dog is a strong creature of habit and because he learns by association, he will soon know there is no other place to relieve himself but the great outdoors.

We take advantage of a very natural instinct of the dog—his desire to keep his sleeping quarters clean (i.e., not to mess his bed). If we can devise a bed that he cannot get out of, then—presto—he is going to stay clean.

The crate is a perfect, natural bed for the dog and a safe, natural spot to place the pet whenever necessary for the dog's safety or the owner's peace of mind. If you are appalled by the idea of confining him to a cage, let me dispel any ideas of cruelty. You are actually catering to a very natural desire on the part of the dog.

Dogs are, and always have been, den and pack animals. Canines naturally and instinctively prefer the shelter of a den. The young are raised in the dens. In his wild state, where does a dog bed down for the night? Does he lie down in the middle of an open field where other animals can pounce on him? No! he finds a cave or the trunk of a tree where he has a feeling of security—a sense of protection. The correct use of a

Since dogs are instinctively den animals, the crate is an ideal tool for housebreaking and a perfect bed for your pet. By nature, he will not mess the area in which he sleeps and he will feel very secure enclosed in the comfort of his simulated "den."

crate merely satisfies the dog's basic need to feel safe, protected, snug and secure.

When thinking of the size of the crate needed for your pup, think small. Think den not condo! If the crate is too large for the puppy, it will encourage the pet to use a small portion for a bed and the remainder as a relief station.

A crate should be large enough for a dog to lie down comfortably, but no larger. Start crate training while you remain in the same room with the crated dog, verbally praising him and letting him know it is pleasing to you that he remains in the crate—quietly. Frequent trips out of the room with quick returns condition the dog to your comings and goings. Gradually extend your absent periods, and in a short time, you can be gone for several hours. While in the crate, the dog should not be scolded. Whining and barking must be ignored. Crate confinement works so well that most dogs soon choose the crate for naps and, in general,

Your dog must be let outside first thing in the morning, as well as several times during the day. A break in this discipline will result in accidents inside the house.

consider it their own private den.

We'll start with the trip out before bedtime. Take the puppy out and give him an opportunity to do his duties. If you are in a protected area let him go free of the leash. Be sure to praise him when he has completed his duties. Take him inside at once and put him in his den.

First thing in the morning (and I mean *first* thing) take the puppy outside. He's been clean all night—and holding it all night—he should do his duty in a hurry. Now bring him in and give him freedom, but in the kitchen only. A child's gate at the kitchen doorway is an excellent barrier to the other rooms in the house. Give him his freedom while breakfast is being prepared and

while you are eating breakfast. After your breakfast, and when you have time to take him out, feed him his breakfast *only leaving the food down for 20 minutes*. After that time, *pick it up*, give him water, *pick it up*, and take him out immediately. Remember the rule—outside after each meal.

Now bring him in and put him in his den and go about your normal routine of the morning. He should stay in the den until about 11:00 to 11:30 a.m. Then take him out of the crate and outside. After he has relieved himself bring him in. While you are preparing and eating lunch, let him have the freedom of the kitchen only for about an hour or two. Give him water, followed by a quick trip outside, and back inside and into the crate until 4:00 p.m. and then outside again.

It is now time to feed him his dinner. I would try to feed him by 4:30 p.m., if possible. As soon as he has finished his last mouthful (remember, leave the food down for 20 minutes) *pick up* his food dish, give him water, and *pick it up,* and take him outside). After he has completed his duties, bring him in and again give him his freedom of the kitchen while you are preparing dinner and during the dinner hour. Give him another trip outside about 8:00 p.m. and again just before your bedtime.

If he does not relieve himself, confine him to the crate. He will soon understand what is expected of him. A long walk before and after he has relieved himself will destroy his understanding of why

If your puppy is going to be trained to "go" indoors, be sure to use an area covered with material not found anywhere else in the house. Your puppy will associate the underfooting with eliminating and "go" only there. Cedar chips are a popular choice because of their odor-removing nature.

Very small breeds of dog, such as the Pug, may be effectively paper trained. This may be the only option for people who live in high-rise apartment buildings or others who cannot get their dog outside readily.

he is being taken outside. Remember to plan a separate exercise period and a separate obedience training period.

IMPORTANT RULES TO FOLLOW:
1. When the pup is out of the crate, he should never be out of sight.
2. Puppies have to relieve themselves after they wake up, after you play with them, and after they eat.
3. Do not vary your puppy's diet. Snacks or treats are forbidden during housebreaking.

ODOR NEUTRALIZERS AND INDOOR SPRAY REPELLENTS
The second phase of housebreaking is getting rid of the pup's past urinary and excretory odors from the house. This is accomplished with an odor neutralizer, which is available in most pet stores and veterinary hospitals. (Do *not* use household cleaners, as they contain ammonia and will attract him back to the same spot. Since dog's urine has ammonia in it, he'll think it's all right to go to the bathroom in that area). Then

Should your puppy accidentally eliminate in the house, it is of utmost importance to permanently remove the odor by using an odor neutralizer or similar product, available at your local pet store. Photo courtesy of Four Paws.

spray the area that has been soiled with an indoor pet spray repellent.

PROPER CORRECTION
The final phase of housebreaking is the technique for correction. *Under no circumstances should the puppy be punished for relieving himself in the house, unless you catch him in the act.* The puppy has no mental capacity to connect your wrath with whatever he did wrong even a few minutes earlier. It is confusing to him and you will only get a puzzled whimper. *Catch him in the act or correction is no good.*

When the dog messes in the house in front of you there is a proper way to correct him. *Do not rub his face in it.* Run over and grab him by the scruff of the neck and shake him. This is exactly what his mother did when he did something wrong. So all you are doing is reinforcing what his mother has already started. This should be accompanied with a harsh "NO!" Immediately take him outside to

Once your dog has found a favorite place to eliminate, he will continue to use that spot—locating it by following his own scent.

finish what he started. This is the only way you can show him what you want. You are catching him in the act, stopping him, taking him outside and then giving him tremendous praise when he finishes.

Many people are mistakenly convinced that a dog messes in the house for spite or revenge, usually for having been left alone. This is incorrect. It is for reasons of anxiety, nervousness or fear that he behaves this way, or simply that he is not properly housebroken. Very often the owner comes home and finds his dog behaving in a fearful, shameful, or generally guilt-ridden manner. It is because of this behavior that the owner is convinced that the dog has messed in the house for spite. It's simply not true. The dog cringes when you come home because he associates your arrival with punishment.

With a little effort on your part and the use of this method the puppy can be housebroken virtually overnight. And don't forget to start obedience training at four months of age. **Good Luck!**

JUMPING ON THE COUNTER

Dogs jump up on tables because it is rewarding. A Dalmatian I know was once rewarded with an entire standing rib roast. It's possible that someone once handed him a treat from the kitchen counter, and dumb as he seems, he remembered. It's just like giving him something from the dinner table—a table is a table. The best way to stop this behavior is not to let it happen in the first place. Don't give your dog any human food at all. Let him eat dog food; that's why they call it dog food!

Once your dog has successfully snatched food from a counter, he must be stopped by means of "counter conditioning" or having a bad experience. This means you have to dream up ways to booby-trap the counter. One way is to tie one end of a piece of string to some pots and pans, and the other end to a ham bone which exists enticingly over the edge of the counter. The dog jumps up on the counter, takes the bone and "Crash!" Here's another trick. Your dog jumps on the counter thinking that it will support him. He'll get a big surprise to find that you've placed a piece of plywood about halfway over the edge of the counter and put those same pots and pans on the board. You get the idea...Then there's the gourmet meal. With some chopped meat, make delicious looking meatballs. They'll be a bit spicy because you'll have mixed in something hot like Chinese mustard or Japanese horseradish (Wasabi). *Caution*: don't use too much; only a little is necessary. Taste it yourself first—you'll see what I mean. Some interesting mats, commonly called scat mats, are on the market, battery-powered or electric. Put one on your counter or table and when your dog touches it, he'll either feel a vibration or a slight shock. You can also buy a dummy mat; as you move the mats to different parts of your home, your dog won't be sure which is the dummy and which will zap him.

The best way to prevent your dog from jumping up on the counter is to never give him human food. However, if your dog has successfully snatched food from the counter, it will be necessary to stop him by using any of several counter-conditioning techniques.

The only way to keep your dog's nose out of the cookie jar is to keep the jar *covered*!

INTRODUCING YOUR DOG TO BABY

Introducing your dog to a new baby will be an easy task if he understands his place in the wolf pack (your family). His lowly position should be clear to him before the baby or anyone else comes to live with you. This is accomplished through obedience training, which should be practiced by every member of the family. Early obedience training will make it much easier for your dog to accept a new baby.

Before your baby arrives, observe your dog's reaction to other babies—in the park, on the street, or in your home. This

Introducing your dog to a new baby should not be difficult if he understands his place in the family. There are a number of preparations you can make to ease the dog's acceptance of a new family member.

will give you an idea of how he will behave when your baby comes home. Does he get excited? Run around like a madman every time you have company? Jump all over everyone? The solution is, *control.* Teach it *before* the blessed event.

I give my clients this advice: buy a life-like doll and dress it in baby clothes, preferably clothes that have been worn by a baby. This will acquaint your dog with those powerful baby aromas. Make a tape recording of a baby crying and play it as often as possible to accustom your dog (and you!) to the sounds of the newborn. Dogs often get concerned when babies cry; they sense (correctly) that a member of the pack is in distress. While the recording is playing, don't run over to the doll, but calmly walk over and pick it up. If your dog remains calm, praise him verbally for being good. "Good" doesn't mean jumping on you to see what you are doing. Let him smell the doll in your arms, on the floor, in the crib. Get him used to these things now.

The introduction of puppy to child almost always results in mutual fun and excitement.

Puppies and children tend to develop instant friendships that last a lifetime. Make sure you teach your children how to properly handle the puppy for both their safety and the puppy's.

dog is calm, give him a treat. This way he will have good feelings about the baby.

Make sure the dog is calm while you gradually introduce him to the baby. If he gets up from a sit or down position, correct him. If you do this for the first week, your dog will develop a good relationship with the baby. Once the dog and baby are acquainted, have the dog lie down while you are taking care of the newborn. Remember, the key to just about every behavior problem in this book is giving your dog exercise and obedience training. That's true for the baby as well as the dog. And, CONGRATULATIONS!

Dogs that have been properly socialized will readily accept a new family member with unabashed enthusiasm. Likewise, children often grow very close to their canine companions, building strong bonds of friendship and trust.

Remember, if you're going to pet the dog, let him earn it by obeying the sit command first.

While the mother is in the hospital, have the father bring home some clothing that the baby has worn. Let the dog sniff it for a day or two before the mother and baby come home.

After the hospital stay, the dog should be greeted without the baby. Have him sit and stay, then pet him. Only praise calm behavior. While the mother or father holds the baby and the

DIGGING

For your dog, digging is a form of exercise, and he needs approximately two hours of exercise per day. If he can play, bark, chew and dig (in the right places), he'll release energy and anxiety, eliminating all kinds of behavior problems, including aggression. Just as your children, and you, need an opportunity to play, so does your dog. So, find the time and get out there with your pet. Play ball or Frisbee; throw a stick for him to chase. Let him release his pent-up energy while making obedience training fun for both of you. After all, you're going to have to train him sooner or later because he is your dog. No one's going to do it for you.

Digging is a natural form of exercise and a stress-releaser for your dog. If your dog is digging in places you don't want him to, then you must either find a place where he can dig or keep him occupied with other activities.

Now, back to digging. Your dog may dig because he sees you doing it and thinks he can do it too. He doesn't know you're planting prize peonies. If you catch him digging, take him by the scruff of the neck and shake him, saying, "No!" at the same time.

Or, buy a hand held air horn at a boating supply store and blow it every time you catch him in the act. He'll soon associate digging with a negative experience. You can also put chicken wire in every hole he digs (dogs hate chicken wire), or you can put granular pet repellent in the holes.

Finally, you can find a place in your yard where he's allowed to dig. Maybe he'll plant his own veggies. Let him know that it's okay for him to dig there by bringing him over to the spot and placing a toy or treat on the ground. Later, put it slightly under the dirt and maybe help him dig. When you catch him digging in the wrong place, correct him and bring him to his spot. Show your approval by praising his digging in the right spot.

Dogs do enjoy digging, but they will also dig to get away from the heat. Make sure your dog has plenty of drinking water when he is outside.

BARKING (INSIDE)

If your dog is barking inside the house, he's probably suffering from separation anxiety; he's not barking from spite or boredom. Do you pet him every time he comes over to you? Does he nudge you to pet him when you're sitting on the couch reading the paper or watching television? It's obvious that he wants you by his side and what he's telling you is to stop what you are doing and pay attention to him. Who's boss anyway? If he wants to be petted, let him earn it by sitting first. Don't indulge your dog.

The easiest solution to barking inside is the same as for barking outside: ignore him. Of course, your neighbors might call the police, in which case, you'll have to resort to other measures.

HE'S OKAY ALONE

Let's say you confine your dog to a crate when you leave the house and then he barks his head off. Try this: about 30 minutes before you leave, give him his Nylabone® (To make a delectable treat, drill small holes in the bone and fill them with peanut butter, cheese spread, or liverwurst. Your dog will keep occupied trying to get at the food.) and then ignore him just as if you were already gone. Don't talk to him, don't say good-bye; just leave. (This also works if you don't leave your dog in a crate). When you return, don't say, "Hi," but walk right past him and ignore him for about ten minutes. Then if he's not barking, take him directly outside to relieve himself. Don't take him out of the crate if he's barking. The rationale behind this is that if you acknowledge him the minute you get home, he'll anticipate your return and bark the entire time you're gone. Your neighbors will surely keep you informed!

Another solution for barking inside is to pretend you are leaving. Place your dog in the crate, put on your coat, take your car keys and actually walk out the door for two minutes. Do it again for five minutes, then ten, then a short period of time, then for hours. If he's quiet when you return, praise him verbally and calmly to let him know what you want. You can even put on the television for him when you're out for a long period. (Perhaps an old Lassie film?)

MAKE THE CRATE GREAT

Why not get him accustomed to the crate and even enjoy it while you are home? Give him his Nylabone® and close the door. If he barks, put a cover over the crate until he stops, then remove it. He'll get the idea.

You could buy an intercom device and when you hear him bark, shout, "NO!" into it. If it's on your front door, either you or your neighbor can shout. "No!" if he barks for no reason.

Never let him out of the crate while he is barking. When he

stops and you finally let him out, take away the Nylabone®. He can only have this chew treat in the crate or when he's alone for a long time.

Another method is to teach your dog to bark on command by getting him excited. When he barks, say, "Speak!" Then, when you want him to stop, say,

is to have the barking cause a bad experience.

Here are some weird and wonderful solutions used by dog professionals: Keep a spray bottle filled with water nearby and whenever the dog barks in the crate, squirt him, then leave the bottle near the crate. The mere sight of it might keep him

Reprimanding your dog for barking inside is not necessarily the way to make him stop, since he may only be trying to get your attention. Try ignoring him instead.

"Enough!" or something similar. This way, the dog will learn to bark on command only.

USE YOUR CREATIVITY

You may come up with some ingenious ways to stop indoor barking. If you do, by all means, let me hear about them. I'm always open to ideas and happy to try new methods. The secret

quiet. Some manufacturers make a device that hooks onto the front of the crate and takes the worry away from you. When the dog barks, it automatically squirts him for half a second.

Finally, and most importantly, give your dog plenty of exercise. That, along with obedience training will help solve a multitude of behavior problems.

BARKING (OUTSIDE)

Dogs bark for various reasons. It's natural, it's fun, and, sooner or later, it's going to get your attention. You can usually tell why your dog is barking. He might bark because someone is on your property. That's his job. He's supposed to warn you if someone is approaching. He might bark because he's frolicking and excited. Chances are you or your kids are roughhousing with him; everyone's noisy and having fun.

IS SOMETHING SCARY HAPPENING?

He might bark because he's afraid of something. Find out what this is. Something really scary could make him bark, or barking might result from conditioned, learned behavior. For example, if your dog is afraid of thunderstorms, and you pet him and talk to him to calm him down, you're playing right into his paws. He'll think you're praising him for his (cowardly) behavior. After all, isn't that what petting is all about? You're actually reinforcing his bad behavior, conditioning him to bark

There are a number of reasons, many of them justified, why your dog barks. However, nuisance barking, or barking for no apparent reason, should be investigated and properly dealt with for your own peace of mind and the consideration your neighbors.

at thunderstorms.

GET HIM USED TO LOUD SOUNDS

For starters, drop a pan (not your steak) across the room from him while he's eating. Don't let it crash right next to him. Try letting water run on a cookie pan while he's eating. Run the vacuum in the next room, then gradually in the same room. Buy a recording of thunder; play it softly at first, then increase the volume. If he is afraid, lower it until he relaxes. Have him lie down for half an hour or an hour. Reward him slowly when he is calm.

DOES HE BARK FOR NO REASON?

Your dog barks when he is outside for the best of reasons. You paid attention to him and brought him into the house the last time he barked. He's no dummy, because he's learned what you taught him!

The best way to stop this outside barking is to ignore him until he realizes barking is futile and he quiets down. If you can't stand the noise or the neighbors are coming with shotguns, go outside and give him a good shake by the scruff of the neck and say, "No!" or hold his muzzle shut and say, "No!" or throw a cup of water in his face and say, "No!"

The only trouble with these solutions to barking is that they provide your dog with the attention he wants. He doesn't care whether he gets positive attention (being brought inside, or given food) or negative attention (being shaken). He has brought you out to him and he thinks that is great. The best thing you can do is to ignore him.

Another way to control barking is to teach him to bark on command, or by "shaping." Encourage him to bark for something he likes; perhaps a toy or a bone. When he sees it and barks for it, say, "Speak!" When he barks, give him the item. Do this over and over, giving him a treat each time he barks on command.

One method of controlling barking is to teach your dog to bark on command. There isn't much you can do to control his slobbering, however.

Then only give him a treat the second or third time, and finally just give him a treat every so often. If he barks without you telling him to speak, correct him by the above method, and say, "Enough!"

Very often the reason your dog is barking is because he needs a way to release energy and he wants to get your attention. If this is the case, try playing a game of fetch in a large open area at least once a day for both exercise and bonding purposes. You may be surprised at the results.

JUMPING UP ON PEOPLE

It's cute when a puppy jumps up on us. We talk to him and pet him and that's a whole lot easier then bending our knees to go down to his level. We know he's trying to get our attention, but we don't care.

Enter the neighborhood Saint Bernard. One friendly jump and you're on the floor. His tail is wagging as he licks your face. This has got to stop.

Here are some techniques to avoid losing face with any dog. They can be combined if you wish. Crouch when a puppy approaches you. He then has no reason to jump up. Or, bring your knees gently into his chest as he jumps, just hard enough to knock him off balance. Grab his front paws and squeeze for a second or two, or hold his front paws as he jumps and move toward him. Dogs hate walking backward. Lightly bump him on the nose with the heel of your hand, or step on his leash giving him just enough slack so when he jumps, he'll be stopped short (this is his doing, not yours).

Let him know that he only gets petted if he sits first. If he gets up while being petted, stop petting him and tell him to sit again. Tell everyone in the household and anyone who visits, not to touch your dog unless he earns it by sitting first.

Whenever your dog jumps up on you, gently raise your knee into his chest. This will make the dog uncomfortable without hurting him and should eventually discourage him from jumping up again.

Although it may have been cute when he was a puppy, your dog's habit of jumping up on people as an adult is annoying, uncomfortable, and possibly dangerous. This inclination should be corrected early in the dog's life.

CHEWING

From three to 12 months of age, puppies chew on everything—your sofa pillows, your newspaper, your neighbor's fingers—everything he can get his teeth on. Although you may think your puppy is doing it out of spite or boredom, he's not. Chewing is natural dog behavior; it relieves tension and anxiety, and it's fun. Besides, puppies simply have to chew because their teeth and gums hurt.

Stop your dog from chewing the wrong things by only allowing him to chew on his own toys. Never give him your old shoes, slippers, or socks—irresistible as they are. Tug-of-war games seem to encourage chewing. Let him chew on his toys and his toys alone.

Nylabone® products are great chew toys for both puppies and older dogs. Nylabones® should be reserved for special occasions—when your dog is in his crate or when he is alone for a long time. When you take him out of the crate, take away the Nylabone®. Confine your dog to a crate whenever you can't keep an eye on him.

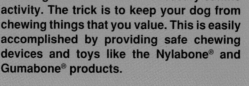

Chewing is a natural and necessary canine activity. The trick is to keep your dog from chewing things that you value. This is easily accomplished by providing safe chewing devices and toys like the Nylabone® and Gumabone® products.

CATCH HIM IN THE ACT

If you think your dog might chew forbidden items when you are not looking, buy a dog repellent from your local pet store or veterinarian. Spray it on those items, then spray your index finger and rub it on his gums. It will taste awful; when he chews on those items, he'll associate them with the bad taste and leave them alone.

Remember, puppies *have* to chew. Even after their adult teeth come in, dogs chew to clean and massage their teeth and gums.

The Plaque Attacker™ bone by Nylabone® has raised dental tips that work wonders in controlling plaque build-up on your dog's teeth.

Gumabones® and Gumabone® flying discs are great for playing fetch with active dogs while also providing a healthy chewing device.

This nylon tug toy by Nylabone® is actually a dental floss. The nylon strands slip between your dog's teeth as he chews or tugs on the toy.

Providing your dog with a Nylabone® is the safest, most effective way of dealing with your dog's chewing needs. Scientific studies have proven that Nylabones® are the longest-lasting and healthiest bones you can buy for your dog.

STOOL EATING (COPROPHAGIA)

Although stool eating is disgusting to us, it seems to be normal behavior for dogs. Puppies like to play with stool, especially if it's frozen. A low protein diet and not enough food are thought to be possible causes of coprophagia. Dogs usually outgrow this habit as they get older.

REPULSIVE BEHAVIOR: WHAT NOT TO DO

Don't walk near the stool and don't flavor the stool with clever seasonings such as hot sauce or peppers. These ideas don't work and could make the dog even more attentive to the tastier stools.

REPULSIVE BEHAVIOR: WHAT TO DO

Sometimes changing a dog's diet and feeding him twice a day will stop coprophagia. Also helpful is cleaning up stool immediately. Ask your veterinarian about products that you can put in your dog's food. While you are talking with him, make an appointment to have a checkup for your pet. You want to be sure he has no medical problems.

Last, but not least, if your dog is eating your cat's stool, either put the litter pan where the dog can't get it, or buy a covered litter box to make it inaccessible.

Promptly cleaning up after your dog helps to avoid parasite infestation as well as stool eating.

CAR SICKNESS

Car sickness usually starts when your dog is a puppy, but if you train him to enjoy riding in a car, it may be avoided. There are several causes of car sickness; the most common are motion of the car, excitement, and anxiety.

Introduce your dog to the car gradually, while he's still young. Don't feed him just before or just after the ride. To accustom him to the car, put him in it and praise him calmly, then take him out and praise him again. Give him a treat if he'll take it. If he's too nervous, he might not. Follow this routine a few times until he begins to relax.

Now, put him back in the car and start the engine. After a minute, turn it off, take the puppy out and play with him. Do this a few times, then take him for a short ride, perhaps halfway down the street. Again play with him afterward. Do this training over an extended period of time when you have the time—not when your boss expects you for dinner.

When the dog becomes calm in the car, take him to the park or to the beach or someplace that's fun for him. If he only rides in the car to get a vaccination at the veterinarian's, or to be dropped off at the boarding kennel, it could be a negative experience.

My dog actually likes the veterinarian and the boarding kennel. The veterinarian pets her, talks to her, and takes the time to become her friend. The kennel personnel also know her and play with her. My dog was introduced to these experiences between seven and 12 weeks of age. If you expose your dog to these situations early in life, it will be easier for both of you as he grows older.

Your dog can easily be trained to enjoy riding in the car. Simply introduce it to him gradually as a puppy and bring him to places that he enjoys, such as the park or the beach. You should not, however, let your dog drive until he has completed driving school and obtained a learner's permit.

The safest way to travel with your dog is to place him in his crate. Besides safety reasons, your dog will feel more comfortable in the security of his living quarters.

Remember to make riding in the car an enjoyable experience. If possible, put him in a crate; he'll be more comfortable than sitting between a couple of rowdy kids. There are even seat belts made for dogs. Make sure the car is not too hot; that would make for a negative experience. And never, never leave your dog in the car with the windows closed in the summer—not even for two minutes. Besides being against the law, your dog could die of heatstroke.

On a long trip, take your dog out of the car every few hours or when you make a gas or bathroom stop. Always keep him on a leash and give him a chance to relieve himself.

It is okay to allow your dog to travel without his crate if he has been trained to be calm and the distance is not too long.

GOING INTO THE TRASH

Dogs love trash because there is food in it! So the best way to keep your dog away from the garbage is to avoid feeding him any human food so he won't go searching for it in the trash. Here are a few more ideas to keep your dog out of the trash. The simplest way is to move the trash out of your dog's reach. Another way is to buy a trash can with a cover that locks.

Here are some more sophisticated ideas. Place a balloon in the can, maybe smeared with bacon grease (sounds good?). When your dog touches it, of course, it will pop, startling him. Or put a small mousetrap in the trash upside down, or another kind of trap that makes a loud noise when touched. Remember the purpose of these gadgets is to train your dog, not to hurt him. There is also a small motion detector that goes off when a dog gets within its range and one that sends off a loud blast if a dog touches the trash. It resets itself automatically.

Be creative, come up with your own ways to booby-trap your pet. Look around, you can find all kinds of things you can use to train your dog. But remember, his experience must be intense for it to work.

The best way to keep your dog from snooping around in the garbage is to avoid feeding him any human food so he won't go searching for it in the trash.

ACKNOWLEDGMENTS

There are so many people that I would like to thank for making my life with dogs a memorable one. It would be impossible to name each and every one—some are deceased and some I've forgotten their names. I would just like to say thanks to all the trainers, veterinarians, clients and dogs that I have known in the past 35 years. Trainers like William B. Dooley, veterinarians like Robert Cohen, D.V.M., and kennel owners like Dick Palazzo of "Purr n Pooch" Kennels. Most of all, I want to thank my wife and friend, Regina, and her dog, Prince the "Wonder Dog." Prince passed away in August, 1995, and he is missed by us every day

Prince the "Wonder Dog" keeping watch over his Princess.